BEI GRIN MACHT SICH IHR WISSEN BEZAHLT

Ruben Picard

Social Networks - Blessing Or Curse?

GRIN Verlag

Bibliografische Information der Deutschen Nationalbibliothek:

Die Deutsche Bibliothek verzeichnet diese Publikation in der Deutschen National-bibliografie; detaillierte bibliografische Daten sind im Internet über http://dnb.d-nb.de/ abrufbar.

Impressum:

Copyright © 2011 GRIN Verlag, Open Publishing GmbH
Druck und Bindung: Books on Demand GmbH, Norderstedt Germany
ISBN: 978-3-640-90923-0

Dieses Buch bei GRIN:

http://www.grin.com/de/e-book/171563/social-networks-blessing-or-curse

GRIN - Your knowledge has value

Der GRIN Verlag publiziert seit 1998 wissenschaftliche Arbeiten von Studenten, Hochschullehrern und anderen Akademikern als eBook und gedrucktes Buch. Die Verlagswebsite www.grin.com ist die ideale Plattform zur Veröffentlichung von Hausarbeiten, Abschlussarbeiten, wissenschaftlichen Aufsätzen, Dissertationen und Fachbüchern.

Besuchen Sie uns im Internet:

http://www.grin.com/

http://www.facebook.com/grincom

http://www.twitter.com/grin_com

Content

1. Introduction

In the past few years a great number of social networks have appeared on the internet. Though the term "social network" seems to be something new, something, associated with the world wide web and new technologies, social networks have existed ever since men have. Any interacting group of people can be considered a social network and is defined by the relationships between the individuals. That makes it really interesting to find a system that was part of our lives from the cradle of humankind, being faced with such a young invention called the internet.

"Facebook", "MySpace", "Twitter", "Bebo", "Xing", "LinkedIn", "StudiVZ" and "Friendster" are just some of these recently established social networks on the internet. What they all have in common is that they try to connect people by providing a platform meant to help users communicate in the most convenient and entertaining way possible or by providing a matchless network service that specialises in a particular area (e.g. music or news).

Today, every fourth internet user is on Facebook[1] - that is half a billion people.[2] A survey I put out concerning the use of social networks by young people in Germany, showed that incredible 88% of the surveyed pupils are signed in on at least one social network and 81% of them log on daily.[3] So if Facebook users were a nation, it would be the third most populated country in the world after China and India (and there are still more users of other social networks) – that is quite astonishing.

I decided to write a research paper about social networks on the internet because I could hardly distinguish whether my own use of such services is either beneficial or reprehensible. These days, new services on the internet that promise to be very entertaining or apparently have a high potential to improve or simplify the way we work and communicate seem to be very attractive to a wide range of internet users. While some people are quite sceptical about online services like social networks, others tend to use them without even considering any potential risks. Are they just blinded by the revolutionary possibilities based on the "Web 2.0"[4] ,or do we actually not have anything to fear?

The social network Facebook will serve as my basic example for the analysis of social networks because it is the most used and thereby most discussed social network on the world wide web; its structure also generally represents other, similar networks.

---

[1] STEINSCHADEN, Jakob: „Phänomen Facebook – Wie eine Website unser Leben auf den Kopf stellt.", Verlag Carl Ueberreuter, Wien 2010, p.7
[2] Ibid. p.12
[3] The corresponding graphs can be found in the addendum, "The Use of The Different Social Networks" & "How Often Do Young People Use Social Networks?"
[4] The term "Web 2.0" describes a new, more interactive Internet that is also more entertaining in comparison to conventional web content.

These social networks are surprisingly entertaining, especially for younger people. But can we trust a completely new way of communication? Considering that almost all social networks are completely free, the question comes up how they can be financed. Do social networks help us organise our lives by providing virtual groups, calendars and event managers? Will these groups even be able to represent political interests? And what about the lack of privacy social networks possibly promote?

Among other aspects, I want to deal with the above-mentioned questions by analysing the way social networks operate and weighing the benefits and disadvantages of social networks on the internet.

2. Introducing Social Networks On The Internet

Social networks on the internet are interactive web services that require a registration. In comparison to conventional web pages, they are similar to computer programs in that users can insert texts, upload photos and videos, and change particular settings. These networks are basically used to communicate with other members.

Users mainly share messages on their own profile page, a section that has the function of a virtual noticeboard. This can also contain links to other websites, and photos and videos in that other members can be tagged. Friends, friends of friends, or any other members can comment on these notes or leave new ones. Who can access one's profile page depends on the privacy settings made. Personal information, a list of friends, and photos and videos of the profile's owner can also be displayed by selecting the according links on the profile page.

Users spend their time by making comments about how they feel and what they are doing, by commenting on others' photos, or just by browsing through other profile pages.

3. Development And Intention Of Social Networks

It was only about ten years ago that the first online social networks as we know them today emerged.[5] The rapid development of such networks did not take place by chance – in fact, it was based on the social network companies' ability to stay flexible, to develop high quality algorithms that were able to structure the mass of data[6] ,and to

---

[5]   WEIGERT, Martin: „Massenphänomen: Die drei Evolutionsstufen sozialer Netzwerke – Social Networks dominieren das Internetgeschehen wie nie zuvor. Wir werfen einen Blick auf die drei Evolutionsstufen sozialer Netzwerke"; http://netzwertig.com/2010/04/21/massenphaenomen-die-drei-evolutionsstufen-sozialer-netzwerke/ ; 21.04.2010 (accessed 04.03.2011)

[6]   Steinschaden 2010, p.13

always come up with new, innovative ideas. Another significant reason is that these social networks could promote themselves just by providing their services that obviously aim to connect people via the internet. So the actual service itself was a way of promoting social networks, and thereby contributed to such a swift expansion of those.

Developers initially aimed to get as many new members as quickly as possible[7] simply by providing a platform that connects its users. But motifs changed over the years and other advancements became more relevant, as I will describe hereafter.

The development of social networks can be divided into "Three Steps Of Evolution Of Social Networks".[8] The first step is considered the "Walled Gardens"[9]-phase. It describes social networks as isolated communities that simply aimed to grow exponentially and were not connected to any other websites or services on the internet. The second phase, launched by Facebook in 2007, gave external website operators the possibility to "enter the walled gardens" by developing little applications to promote their interests. In this phase, the social networks started to develop *application programming interfaces*[10]. To a certain degree, it was now possible to surf specific web content, without even leaving the network site. Of course that brought along the side effect that users spent more and more time on these websites, so other social network operators tried to follow Facebook's innovation.

The third phase – "The Whole Web As A Platform"[11] – that began about two years ago emphasises the social network companies' altered motifs that I mentioned before. Only Facebook and Twitter[12] ever successfully reached this phase, while others are more or less struggling to catch up. In that last phase, major network services try to be part of the whole internet. Again Facebook played the pioneer's role – its developers introduced the "Like-Button", a small piece of universal software (a "plugin"[13]) that can be easily attached to a website to give visitors the opportunity to "like" the provided service or particular contents of it simply by clicking on this little button.

> (...) it does not seem too unusual hearing Mike Schroepfer, Vice President of Engineering for Facebook, say: 'It is quite possible, that one day there will be no thing called Facebook.com any more.'[14]

---

[7] Weigert 2010
[8] Ibid.
[9] Ibid. (meaning a bounded domain)
[10] A programming interface that allows external programmers to integrate their own software into another system (also called: API).
[11] Weigert 2010
[12] A social network service on the internet that specialises in news.
[13] A set of software components that adds functionality to another, larger piece of software (e.g. a website).
[14] Steinschaden 2010, p.34

At first sight this quotation is pretty misleading, but it constitutes exactly what Facebook and other networks also try to be: The part of the internet that links any websites to the own social network and thereby provides some kind of an evaluation system (because visitors can "like" or comment what they come across) – a *database of interests* that can be pretty valuable when it comes to marketing strategies of advertisers.[15] So in the end, besides the intention to expand the particular social network, there is the goal of collecting as much information as possible about users and their preferences. That is not too obvious and maybe even scary to a certain degree.

4. How Social Networks Influence Our Lives

Using a social network on the internet is certainly more complex than it seems. In reality, there is a certain number of people we can develop a meaningful relationship with – according to Robin Dunbar[16], a group of approximately 150 people. Obviously there is a connection between us and every single individual out of these 150. We might just call them friends, but they can be colleagues, partners, fellows, etc. as well. They talk to each other, they share recommendations, and they suggest to each other to do something or not to do it. But if we think this is the amount of people we can seriously influence and we can also seriously be influenced by, we commit a major fault.

> *Our (...) research has shown that the spread of influence in social networks obeys what we call the Three Degrees of Influence Rule. Everything we do or say tends to ripple trough our network, having an impact on our friends (one degree), our friends' friends (two degrees), and even our friends' friends' friends (three degrees). Our influence gradually dissipates and ceases to have a noticeable effect on people beyond the social frontier that lies at three degrees of separation. Likewise, we are influenced by friends within three degrees but generally not by those beyond*[17]

Christakis, Nicholas & Fowler, James; London 2011

This concept shows that we are not influenced by roughly 150 people in our social

---

[15] This will be discussed more extensively in „5. Business of social networks", p.8
[16] KROTOSKI, Aleks: „Robin Dunbar: We can only ever have 150 friends at most... - Evolutionary anthropologist Robin Dunbar tells Aleks Krotoski why even Facebook cannot expand our true social circle: our brains just aren't big enough to cope", 14.03.2010 (accessed 09.03.2011) http://www.guardian.co.uk/technology/2010/mar/14/my-bright-idea-robin-dunbar (Also from the video on that page)
[17] CHRISTAKIS, Nicholas & FOWLER, James: „Connected – The Amazing Power of Social Networks and How They Shape Our Lives", HarperCollinsPublishers (first published in 2010), London 2011, p. 27-28

network of friends, but rather by up to 3.375.000 people (to make it simple, I assume the individuals do not know each other), of whom we have only seen a few in our lives. Of course we are mutually influenced the most by our friends, less by our friends' friends and logically least by our friends' friends' friends.[18] It is pretty interesting that the average number of friends a user has on social networks on the internet (130 friends) is so close to the number Robin Dunbar stated for real social networks. That suggests that his theory is applicable to online social networks as well.[19]

Illustration Of The Three Degrees Of Influence Rule

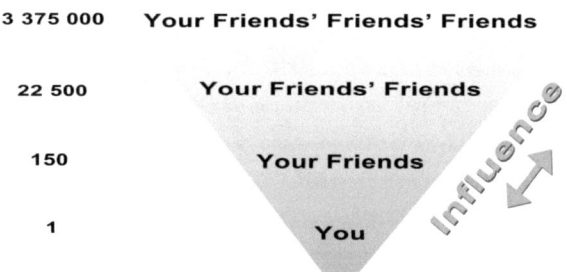

So now, when we transfer these scientific circumstances to the use of social networks, their influence on our lives becomes clear.

When users of social networks type in their comments, most of them think that these more or less important messages will be read by some of their friends and maybe by a couple of their friends' friends. For them it is rather hard to imagine that this comment can even influence their third-degree-friends.

A study conducted by Christakis & Fowler pointed out that somebody is 15% more likely to be happy when he is directly connected to someone who is happy (the same applies for second-degree-friends with a chance of 10% and for third-degree-friends with a chance of 6%). So we can actually "share"[20] our feelings by writing a comment and thereby influence our friends within three degrees – as well as we can be influenced.

When users share a comment they provide exactly the same information for hundreds, thousands, or even half a billion people[21]. In real life, they would only share this with a

---

[18] Ibid. p.28
[19] Steinschaden 2010, p.71
[20] Meaning not only to write, but to actually share them.
[21] Depending on the privacy settings. Also discussed in „2. Introducing Social Networks On The

couple of friends.[22] It is a bit as if we would run through our village telling everybody that *"we are having a good time"* or that *"we will go to sleep now"*. Users are confronted with a huge public and obviously they can not cope with it. That is absolutely human, because usually no one learns how to handle such a wide public except for politicians or celebrities. Detractors say that a social pressure develops that urges members to live compliant and to not raise their voices if they disagree with something, because everything we utter will be evaluated and can be used against us.[23]

Another habit social networks on the internet initiated is the urge to share what we are doing or what just happened to us. Users want to be the first to report *"that there was a crash on the main road just in front of their house"* or that they *"bought that new mobile phone"*, for instance. As long as it is intriguing, controversial, or of any public interest, it has to be shared. A user can easily "be urged to behave like a medium and to submit stories, others will appreciate."[24] A competition emerges, because members want to show off with the best stories and want to have as many friends as possible.[25]

It is far too simple to say that online social networks are just a virtual way of communication and that they represent a common, face to face chat. They unconsciously urge us to offer the information others want to hear and to deal with a greater quantity of people, as we actually can cope with.

5. Business Of Social Networks

Almost all social networks on the internet are free, but Facebook's 60.000 servers, server spaces in foreign countries, and 1400 employees are not cheap.[26] Somehow social networks must have an income, considering that they even make a profit.

The major revenue of social network services is made with advertisements – the most popular way of making money on the internet. Because advertisers have specific target groups for what they offer, for them it is very lucrative to make use of social networks' stored information about users. Or as Jakob Steinschaden, a young and committed writer who made several investigations about the "Web 2.0", phrased it:

Internet"
[22] Steinschaden 2010, p.158-160
[23] Steinschaden 2010, p.160
[24] Steinschaden 2010, p.177
[25] Ibid.
[26] Ibid. p.39

*That is every market researcher's dream: consumers voluntarily give an
unfiltered report about their everyday life in an electronic and thereby
machine-readable way.*[27]

Steinschaden, Jakob; 2010

Advertisers pay a lot of money for these *targeted advertisements*[28] on social network
pages[29] and apparently it is profitable for them.

It is not even a juridical issue, because social networks do not actually make personal
data available for third parties. They just give advertisers the opportunity to let their
advertisements be displayed on specific profile pages. Assuming a handbag maker
wants his advertisement for a fancy new handbag to be seen by young French women
that are interested in fashion and aged 17-25, he can just type in the according criteria
and do so. His advertisement will appear on all the pages that meet these criteria.

For users it is almost impossible to see through this devious system: They voluntarily
provide a variety of information about their lives that advertisers use to make aligned
advertisements on their profile pages. Social networks are the interlink between
advertisers and potential customers, and that is what they get paid for.

6. Weighing The Benefits And Disadvantages Of Social Networks

6.1 The Potential Of Social Networks

"A woman whose three-year-old son was abducted and taken to live in Hungary has
been reunited with him 27 years later after finding his name on Facebook."[30] This is just
one of the heart-warming stories about reunion and reconciliation thanks to the use of
social networks that are frequently brought to us. Nevertheless it is pretty admirable
what social networks are capable of.

The most useful function of social networks are virtual groups that link an event with all
the people involved. They can informally give feedback whether they will attend, will not
attend, or will maybe attend. Furthermore they can express their ideas, doubts, or any
other comments on it, and the attendees do not have to be called one by one if there is
an amendment to the event. So it is favourable for clubs and organisations to set up
such groups. They replace external websites and there is no need to have any
advanced computer skills to construct them, too. Therefore social networks do help us

---

[27] Ibid. p.125
[28] „Targeted advertising" is an advertising method that aims to reach a specific group of people.
[29] Steinschaden 2010, p.126
[30] DE BRUXELLES, Simon: "Facebook reunites mother with long-lost son"; 30.05.2009
      (accessed 13.03.2011) http://www.timesonline.co.uk/tol/news/uk/article6386101.ece

to get organised and we can save time if we use them.

Because it is very easy to find like-minded people on social networks[31], it is even possible that such groups could serve as some sort of political lobby that highlights certain demands of a certain group of people. But it is arguable if these groups represent actual interests or if they may be distorted due to opportunistic behaviour.[32]

6.2 Dangers Of The Use Of Social Networks

6.2.1 Consequences Of Giving Personal Information

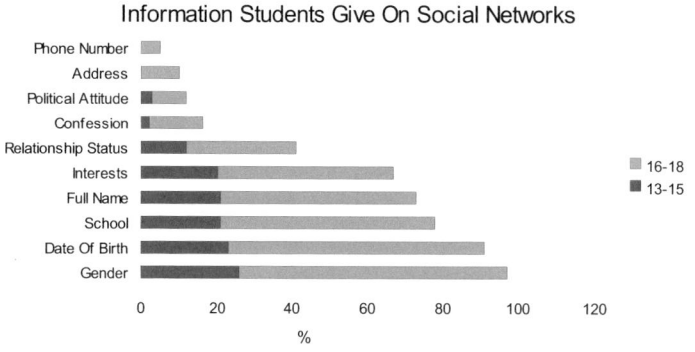

A survey I conducted concerning the information students give on social networks, showed that 73% of the surveyed pupils gave their full name, 91% gave their date of birth, 97% gave their gender, 78% indicated the school they go to, and 67% gave at least some personal interests. It also showed that students aged 16-18 are more willing to give their personal information whereas students at the age of 13-15 give less. Disregarding that these information are used to make targeted advertisements[33], this is what the majority of teenagers allow others to know about their lives – pretty much, considering that they would not tell them if they were asked on the streets. Again it depends on the privacy settings made whether one can access these information or not. The majority of users do not make their profile page accessible for all other members, but a lot of them allow their friends' friends to do this, because they think that only closely related people can view their profile page then. Unfortunately they do not expect this to be approximately 16 900 people (Assuming a user has 130 friends and

---

[31] Steinschaden 2010, p.155-156
[32] Referring to "4. How Social Networks Influence Our Lives"; p.6
[33] Referring to "5. The Business Of Social Networks" p.8

the individuals do not know each other).[34] Furthermore some members do not know how to make their information only available for friends, or they do not care about it because they do not see any potential risks in using a social network.[35]

So how can users be so careless with their personal data on the internet while they usually tend to be careful with this in real life? It is quite likely that there are potential criminals among these 16 900 – at least there will be several among all users of a particular social network. Especially younger members are in danger of getting (sexually) harassed, either via the internet, or in real life because they even agree to meet strangers. Unfortunately their parents hardly ever check what they are doing on the internet and who they are in contact with.

6.2.2 No Privacy

Multimedia content makes social networks entertaining, but the possibility to upload photos and videos poses a risk. Not only because they can be private, but also because it is hard to really delete them. Though users can stop making them appear on the social network website, social networks are still entitled to save these photos and videos as long as this is declared in the terms of use.[36] But similar to other web services users can usually not be bothered to read them.

Today many people own a digital camera, so they take some pictures on almost every event they attend. Younger people may even have a "smart phone"[37] with internet access, so they can upload a picture right after they took it. Users mainly upload pictures because they want to give others the opportunity to share their impressions. But the majority does not care whether the people on these pictures want to be seen on the internet. Some of them deliberately upload unfavourable pictures to harm others.

Potential employers more and more frequently type in the names of their applicants before they even read their application. If they find any unpleasant photos of the applicant (e.g. of him together with drunken people) they will certainly not hire them. The Problem is that someone who is not signed in on the same social networks as the one who has taken pictures, can not even control whether there are also pictures of him that he does not want to be on the internet.

"In a frank and transparent world, so his (Mark Zuckerberg's) assumption, the people

---

[34] Steinschaden 2010, p.158
[35] A corresponding graph can be found in the Addendum, " Is The Use Of Social Networks Potentially Dangerous?"
[36] This applies to the majority of social network services.
[37] The term „smart phone" describes mobile phones that have a camera, internet access, and other entertainment features.

would act more honest and be forced to take responsibility for their behaviour."[38] This is what Mark Zuckerberg, founder of Facebook, thinks about his online service and its privacy issues. He sounds as if he believes that there is no need of privacy, and it is surprising that younger social network users generally agree with him. Though this notion must be accepted, I would like to cite Thomas W. Malone from a conversation with Jakob Steinschaden in contrast. He is a renowned professor of the Massachusetts Institute of Technology in Cambridge.

> *Too little privacy (...) becomes a problem: Because when I know that everybody can know everything I say, there will be many things that I will never say.*[39]
>
> *Thomas W. Malone in a conversation with Jakob Steinschaden; 2010 in "Phänomen Facebook"*

In the end, we undergo a revolution that will make us lose our privacy due to the use of social networks. If this is going to be a bad progression or not that remains to be seen.

7. Conclusion

Social networks are both a technical and a social revolution. They enable us to communicate with (long forgotten) friends from all over the earth and to easily organise events – also they can be very entertaining. The question is if we have to sacrifice our privacy and dignity to use them over time, and if we will learn to develop relationships with a wider public of much more than 150 people. More obvious is the question if targeted advertisement on social networks will remain profitable enough to finance them. Considering that social networks recently started to incorporate whereabouts into their services[40], I wonder whether users will still tolerate upcoming innovations that will claim more and more details of their private lives.

Eventually social networks on the internet are rapidly developing services that will require careful observation, so that we are always able to decide whether they enrich or deteriorate our lives.

---

[38] Steinschaden 2010, p.158
[39] THOMAS W. MALONE in a conversation with Jakob Steinschaden; "Phänomen Facebook"; 2010; p.161
[40] Referring to „Facebook Places", a technical innovation that enables users to share their location.

Bibliography

Books

CHRISTAKIS, Nicholas & Fowler, James: "Connected – The Amazing Power of Social Networks and How They Shape Our Lives", HarperCollinsPublishers
(first published in 2010), London 2011

GÖRIG, Carsten: "Gemeinsam Einsam – Wie Facebook, Google & Co. unser Leben verändern", Orell Füssli Verlag AG, Zürich 2011

STEINSCHADEN, Jakob: "Phänomen Facebook – Wie eine Website unser Leben auf den Kopf stellt", Verlag Carl Ueberreuter. Wien 2010

Internet Sources

DE BRUXELLES, Simon: "Facebook reunites mother with long-lost son";
30.05.2009 (accessed 13.03.2011);
http://www.timesonline.co.uk/tol/news/uk/article6386101.ece

DWORSCHAK, Manfred: "Das Netz im Netz";
22.11.2010 (accessed 06.03.2011);
http://www.spiegel.de/spiegel/print/d-75261513.html

HEFFERNAN, Virginia: "Magic and Loss"; 18.02.2011 (accessed 16.03.2011);
http://www.nytimes.com/2011/02/20/magazine/20FOB-Medium-t.html

JOHSON, Steven: "How Twitter Will Change the Way We Live", 05.06.2009
(accessed 05.03.2011);
http://www.time.com/time/printout/0,8816,1902604,00.html

KENNEDY, Dan: "The trouble with Faceook – the crisis sparked by Facebook's abandonment of privacy could be its downfall – but where would its users go instead?";
18.05.2010 (accessed 06.03.2011);
http://www.guardian.co.uk/commentisfree/cifamerica/2010/may/18/facebook-privacy

KROTOSKI, Aleks: "Robin Dunbar: We can only ever have 150 friends at most... Evolutionary anthropologist Robin Dunbar tells Aleks Krotoski why even Facebook cannot expand our true social circle: our brains just aren't big enough to cope";
(Also from the video on that page); 14.03.2010 (accessed 09.03.2011);
http://www.guardian.co.uk/technology/2010/mar/14/my-bright-idea-robin-dunbar

LISCHKA, Konrad: "Facebook greift nach der Web-Herrschaft", 22.04.2010
(accessed 06.03.2011);
http://www.spiegel.de/netzwelt/web/0,1518,druck-690506,00.html

LISCHKA, Konrad: "Web-Erfinder warnt vor Facebooks Datenmonopol"; 20.11.2010
(accessed 06.03.2011);
http://www.spiegel.de/netzwelt/web/0,1518,730259,00.html

PARK, Alice: "Feeling Alone Together: How Loneliness Spreads"; 01.12.2009
(accessed 04.03.2011);
http://www.time.com/time/health/article/0,8599,1943748,00.html

PFLITSCH, Andreas: "Facebook-Revolte – Die Ägypter haben es vorgemacht"
14.02.2011 (accessed 10.03.2011);
http://www.tagesspiegel.de/kultur/facebook-revolte-die-aegypter-haben-es
vorgemacht-/3814842.html

SIMMONS, Andy: "How To Click and Clean Your Online Profiles"; Reader's Digest April
2008 (accessed 09.03.2011); http://www.rd.com/money/dangers-of-social-networks/

RICHTEL, Matt & HELFT Miguel: "Facebook Users Who Are Under Age Raise
Concerns" 11.03.2011 (accessed 17.03.2011);
http://www.nytimes.com/2011/03/12/technology/internet/12underage.html

STENGEL, Richard: "Only Connect"; 15.12.2010 (accessed 09.03.2011);
http://www.time.com/time/specials/packages/article/0,28804,2036683_2037181_20371
79,00.html

WEIGERT, Martin: "Massenphänomen: Die drei Evolutionsstufen sozialer Netzwerke
Social Networks dominieren das Internetgeschehen wie nie zuvor. Wir werfen einen
Blick auf die drei Evolutionsstufen sozialer Netzwerke";
21.04.2010 (accessed 04.03.2011);
http://netzwertig.com/2010/04/21/massenphaenomen-die-drei-evolutionsstufen
sozialer-netzwerke/

Newspaper Articles

RICHTEL, Matt: "Wired for Distraction – Struggling to Learn in a Flood of Texting, Web
Surfing and Games", 29.11.2010, Redwood City, California
The New York Times, on the cover page and on page 4

Addendum

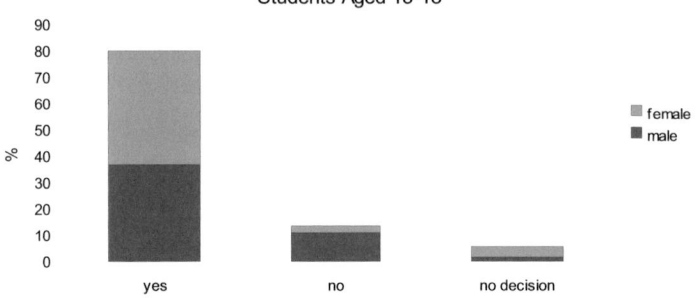

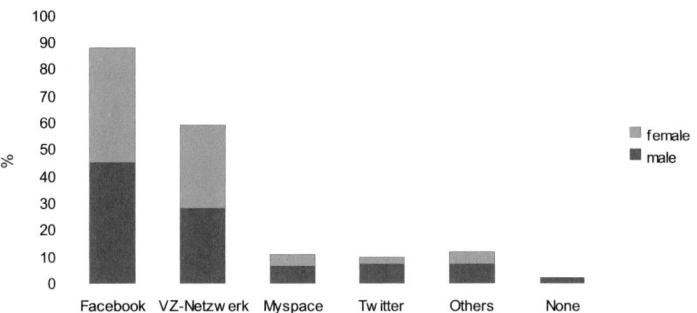

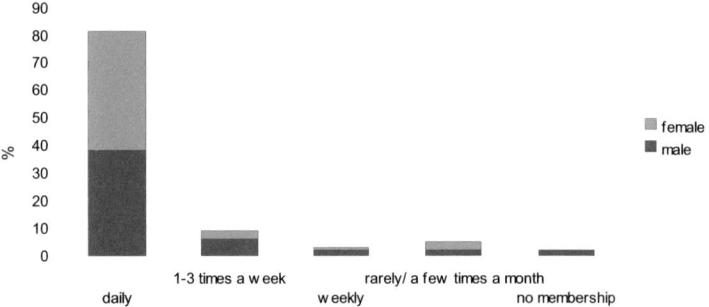